Thoughts
to Make Your
Heart
Sing

Thoughts to Make Your Heart Sing

Written by SALLY LLOYD-JONES

Illustrated by JAGO

ZONDERKIDZ

Thoughts to Make Your Heart Sing
Copyright © 2012 by Sally Lloyd-Jones
Illustrations © 2012 by Jago
This title is also available as a Zondervan ebook.
Visit www.zondervan.com/ebooks
Requests for information should be addressed to:
Zonderkidz, *Grand Rapids, Michigan 49530*

ISBN: 978-0-310-72163-5

Art direction: Cindy Davis
Cover and interior design: Brooke Reynolds
Theological review: Kathy Keller, MA Theological Studies, Gordon-Conwell Seminary
Printed in China

13 14 15 16 17 18 19 20 /LPC/ 12 11 10 9 8 7 6 5

ACKNOWLEDGMENTS

I have been inspired and taught by many great Christian theologians, writers, and teachers, among them: C. S. Lewis, Helmut Theilke, Corrie ten Boom, Amy Carmichael, David Martyn Lloyd-Jones, Jonathan Edwards, Brennan Manning, Timothy Keller, and John Stott. I am grateful for each of them. Some of them are quoted in these pages.

Most of all I am grateful to my parents, to whom I dedicate this book. They gave me the greatest gift a parent could give: an invitation to Faith—what Corrie ten Boom called the "Fantastic Adventure In Trusting Him."

My prayer is that the reader will find these thoughts an invitation to join the same Fantastic Adventure.

FOREWORD

When I first heard that Sally Lloyd-Jones was writing a book of devotional thoughts for children, I was intrigued. Now that I have seen it, I am delighted.

Why has so little attention ever been given to the devotional lives of children? Of course we should be doing all the standard things: teaching them the catechism, including them in family devotions, helping them to participate in worship. But encouraging a child to develop his or her own devotional life has long been a missing piece that has direct effect on whether a child grows up with a balanced spiritual life or one that is dangerously one sided.

By that I mean that it is all too easy to concentrate on data-transmission to our children. Of course, laying down a foundation of biblical truths, Bible memorization, and doctrinal basics is very important.

Somehow, however, the experiential side of a relationship with God is often neglected, so that by the time children are teens, they are woefully lopsided—long on information, but short on experience of God's presence.

While one book is not enough by itself to correct this imbalance, *Thoughts to Make Your Heart Sing* may be the best, first introduction for children to have their own time with Jesus. It shares the same whimsical art as *The Jesus Storybook Bible*—one of my favorite gifts to friends, whether they have children or not—as well as Sally's easy-to-understand prose.

Best of all, it is saturated with an understanding of the Gospel, God's love freely given to us, but purchased by Jesus.

Although designed for children, these are thoughts that should make all of our hearts sing.

AUTHOR NOTE

These thoughts are to remind you of things that are true.

They aren't meant to be read all at once—just one a day.

They come from the Bible—the place where God has told you all these magnificent things about how he loves you and how you can love him.

Sometimes I wrote for people who already know what it is to come home to God. Other times I wrote for people who are just finding out.

You listen to whatever God wants to say to you.

SALLY

"Satisfy us each morning with your unfailing love,
so we may sing for joy to the end of our lives."
PSALM 90:14 (NLT)

TABLE OF CONTENTS

TABLE OF CONTENTS

TABLE OF CONTENTS

DANCE!

In the beginning, God sang everything into being—for the joy of it—and set the whole universe dancing.

God was in the center, at the heart of everything.

Like the dance of the planets before the sun—turning, spinning, circling, wheeling, revolving, orbiting around and around— God made everything in his world and in his universe and in his children's hearts to center around him—in a wonderful Dance of Joy!

It's the Dance you were born for.

"The morning stars sang together, and all the sons of God shouted for joy." **JOB 38:7 (KJV)**

CATACLYSM!

What if the planets put themselves at the center instead of the sun?

CATACLYSM!

The Bible says that's what it was like when we sinned.

God made his children's hearts to join together in the wonderful Dance of Joy—orbiting and circling around him. But we put ourselves in the center instead of God. We put ourselves in God's place—which is what sin is.

It broke God's perfect world. And now our hearts are out of step with God and the universe and each other and our own selves.

But God had a Plan.

And a Rescuer.

One day Jesus would come to take the cataclysm of our sin into his own heart.

And lead us back into the Dance of Joy.

"You will again be happy and dance."
JEREMIAH 31:4 (NLT)

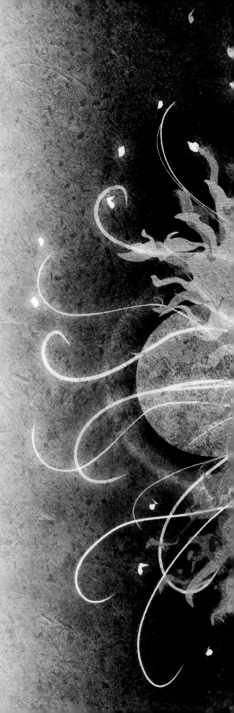

LOVING HEAVENLY FATHER

God tells us he is the Creator of Heaven and Earth! The Mighty God!

And says he is a father as well—your Father.

And then he shows us a tender picture—like a snapshot from his camera. It's of our God teaching you—his little child—how to walk. Taking you in his arms. Gently leading you.

All through your life—from beginning to end—God himself teaches you how to walk with him.

He leads you by the hand.

" ... I myself taught my people how to walk, leading them along by the hand." **HOSEA 11:3** (paraphrase based on NLT)

THREE SMALL WORDS

"[Treasure] these words of mine in your heart and in your soul." **DEUTERONOMY 11:18 (ESV)**

What words does God want you to treasure in the deepest part of you?

"Be good"? "Do it better"? "Try harder"? Are those the words God wrote in the Bible for us, to rescue and free us?

No. Those words only show us what we can't do.

The words God wants us to remember are just three small ones: "I love you!"

They are the words that stop the Terrible Lie that Satan whispered to Eve in the garden: "God doesn't love you!" They are the words that heal the poison in our hearts that stops us from trusting God.

They are the words that Jesus came to tell us with his whole life.

They are the words he died to prove.

What words will you treasure today?

IN ALL THE EARTH!

Of all the incredible things God made,
which do you think is the most amazing?

Is it the Grand Canyon? Or the Milky Way?
What about the North Pole?

Or Mount Everest? Or sunsets? Or starfish?
Or the cheetah?

Do you know what God says is the best, most magnificent, incredible thing he has ever made?

You.

"You will be my own special treasure ... though all the earth is mine." **EXODUS 19:5** *(paraphrase)*

SING YOUR SONG!

The whole world is singing a song. Have you heard it?

The wind is whispering it in the trees. The rain is dancing it on the rooftops. The whole of creation is singing it out together: "God loves us. He made us. He's very pleased with us!"

It's the song that's been sung since the beginning. The song God created everything in his world to sing.

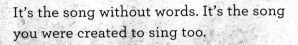

It's the song without words. It's the song you were created to sing too.

We forgot our song long ago, when we turned and ran away from God. But Jesus has come to bring us home to God—and give us back our song.

So go on—sing your song!

"Shout with joy to the Lord, all the earth! Come before him, singing with joy … He made us, and we are his." **PSALM 100:1–3 (NLT)**

GOD IN HEAVEN

It was never meant to be this way.

When the first human beings, Adam and Eve, ran from God, they broke his heart and his world—and tears and sickness and pain and death came in.

God made his world to be our perfect home. But sin has spoiled everything. We have made a terrible mess of God's world. We lost it all!

Did God abandon us? Did he just look down from heaven at the mess we made?

No. He didn't just look down. He came down. God himself came down.

Not as a judge to punish us, but as a Rescuer to save us.

"He reached down from heaven and rescued me."
PSALM 18:16 (NLT)

CHARGE!

What is sin? Sin is trying to get away from God who loves us—it's wanting to go our own way without him.

But the Bible says it's not like simply wandering off the path and getting lost by mistake. It's like a horse charging at full speed away from him. We want to get away from God that badly! We are like horses galloping headlong after the things we want.

But God can stop runaway horses.

And lead them gently back.

"Is anyone sorry for doing wrong? ... No! All are running down the path of sin as swiftly as a horse galloping ..." **JEREMIAH 8:6 (NLT)**

WINKIE

During World War II, a damaged plane crashed into the sea. The crew had no way to radio for help, but they had a vital piece of equipment: a pigeon named—Winkie!

Winkie flew all the way home to the base— all 129 miles—alerting rescuers and saving the entire crew. She was awarded a special medal for her heroism.

However far away they are, birds can find their way home again and again and again. But not God's children—God's children aren't homesick for him.

God is our true home. Away from him, we are lost.

Are you far away today? Be like Winkie. The minute you realize you've gone off course, head home.

"Oh, return to me, for I have paid the price to set you free." ISAIAH 44:22 (NLT)

COME BACK!

God just wants us close to him. Whenever
we wander away from him, he says to us:

> Come back to me
> Because I am gentle and kind.
>
> I'm slow to become angry with you
> But very quick to forgive you!
>
> So come back home to me
> And be sorry inside your heart.
>
> I'm waiting to forgive you.
>
> Wherever you are,
> Whatever you've done,
> Just come!

"'Even now,' declares the Lord, 'return to me with
all your heart … Return to the Lord your God, for he
is gracious and compassionate, slow to anger and
abounding in love.'" **JOEL 2:12–13 (NIV)**

COVENANT GOD

A covenant in the Bible was an unbreakable contract—written not in ink but in blood.

You'd kill an animal and say, "If I don't keep my promise, let me die like this animal!"

God made a covenant like that with his children and said, "I will ALWAYS love you!" We were supposed to promise, "We'll always love you too!"

But we ran from God and broke our side of the contract. And the law called for our deaths. And yet God spared us. How? Did he just ignore the law? No.

God himself kept our side of the covenant for us—and, in Jesus, died instead of us.

God's promise to always love us is written in blood—the blood of his son.

[Jesus said,] "This is my blood, which confirms the covenant between God and his people."
MATTHEW 26:26, 28 (NLT)

HARDLY-EVEN-THERE FAITH

When Jesus's friends asked, "Give us more faith!", Jesus told them they already had enough.

Even faith as small as a mustard seed is enough. How small is a mustard seed? About as small as the period at the end of this sentence. Jesus said that's enough faith to uproot a huge tree and plant it into the sea!

Even the tiniest speck of faith—the little bit you have—so-small-it's-hardly-even-there faith—is enough. Enough for you to do whatever Jesus has asked you to do.

Because it's not about us and how much faith we have.

It's about him and how faithful he is!

"If you have faith as small as a mustard seed, you can say to this mulberry tree, 'Be uprooted and planted in the sea,' and it will obey you." **LUKE 17:6 (NIV)**

FRIEND OF SINNERS

One day, Jesus visited the important city of Jericho and had a meeting.

Who with? The mayor? The bishop?

No. Jesus made a beeline straight for ... the biggest sinner he could find. (Who, by the way, was quite small and up a tree.)

It would be like going to Washington D.C. and instead of having tea with the president, finding the worst criminal and having tea with him.

Zacchaeus was the most hated, despised man in the whole city and—of all people— he was the one Jesus chose to have tea with. (Back then that was scandalous— it was like saying, "Let's be friends!")

The Important People sneered, "Jesus is the friend of sinners!"

They were right. Jesus loves sinners.

And they're the whole reason he came.

"Christ Jesus came into the world to save sinners."
1 TIMOTHY 1:15 (NLT)

FREE GIFT

Zacchaeus was a big sinner. He stole, cheated, lied—why would Jesus love him? Did Zacchaeus say, "I'll be a better person", and that's why Jesus wanted to be his friend?

No. It was entirely the other way around.

Even when no one else wanted anything to do with Zacchaeus, even before Zacchaeus mended his ways, Jesus was his friend. Jesus accepted him and loved him.

Zacchaeus didn't have to do anything to make Jesus love him. And neither do you. Because, you see, God's love is a free gift. You can't earn it. You don't deserve it. You can't pay for it.

You need only open your hands to receive it.

"God saved you by his grace when you believed. And you can't take credit for this, it is a gift from God."
EPHESIANS 2:8 (NLT)

FAR, FAR AWAY

When God says he forgives us, he is saying,
"I've sent all the wrong things you ever
did far, far away from me. I've hurled them
away where no one can ever look on them—
not even me!"

Where is the farthest place you've ever
traveled? God has sent your sins farther.

What's the farthest place you can even
imagine? Galaxies twelve billion light
years away?

God sends your sins even farther away
than that! You won't ever see them again.

"He has removed our sins as far from us as the east
is from the west." **PSALM 103:12 (NLT)**

BLESS YOU!

[God said,] "I will surely bless you." **GENESIS 22:17 (NIV)**

People say, "Bless you!" when you sneeze.
"Bless" has turned into a bit of a feeble word.

But in the Bible it's much stronger.
(And it has nothing to do with sneezing!)

When God promises to bless you, he is saying,
"I'm going to make you into everything I ever
meant for you to be!"

It means God is taking every day and every single thing that happens in it—good or bad—to make you stronger, to mend whatever is broken inside, to change you into the person you were always meant to be.

Just as a caterpillar is totally changed into a butterfly, being blessed means being totally transformed.

God is transforming everything—his broken world—and you.

GOD'S LITTLE FINGER

King David was marveling at God's universe.

"When I look at your heavens, the work of your
fingers, the moon and the stars, which you have set
in place, what is man that you are mindful of him …?"
PSALM 8:3–4 (ESV)

But he didn't say God made the universe
with his arm—or even his hand. He said,
"God, you made it with your fingers!"

The vast universe is so small to God that
for him it's like making a toy model—with
just his fingers!

If the Milky Way galaxy were the size of
North America, our solar system would be
a coffee cup, and earth would be a speck of
dust inside the cup.

The universe is tiny to God!

What are human beings next to God?
Nothing.

And yet God says you fill his mind.

GLORIFY!

God tells us to glorify him. "Glorify" means "to make a big deal of." When someone makes a big deal of you, it fills up your heart with joy.

But why does God need us to make a big deal of him? Why does he need us to get joy?

He doesn't. In the beginning God the Father and Jesus, his Son, together with the Holy Spirit, were already there—a loving family, glorifying each other in this wonderful Dance of Joy.

No. God didn't create us so he could get joy—he already had it.

He created us so he could share it.

He knows it's the thing your heart most needs to be happy. When God says, "Glorify me!", he's really saying, "Be filled with Joy!"

He's inviting us into his Forever Happiness.

"His secret purpose framed from the very beginning [is] to bring us to our full glory" 1 CORINTHIANS 2:7 (NEB)

GOD'S RULES

God's rules are his gift to us. To help us be who we are really are.

But God doesn't want you thinking that if you keep the rules you'll make him love you.

He wants you to rely on Jesus's record, not yours—because Jesus has already done everything the rules required.

You obey God, not so that God will love you—He already does. He couldn't love you any more than he does!—but because you love him.

We can love God's rules now—because they show us more about God and how to love him.

"For God is working in you, giving you the desire and the power to do what pleases him."
PHILIPPIANS 2:13 (NLT)

SECRET WEAPON

Did you know God has armed all of his children with a secret weapon?

The whole universe was made by it! It can turn darkness into light!

What is it? A sharp sword—the Word of God.

You can use it on your fears. Instead of listening to what your fears are saying, and believing them, you can pick up the sword of God's Word and go on the attack.

How do you do that?

You say these things that are true—the things
God has told you: "God has a good plan for my
life!" "I will trust and not be afraid!" "Through
Jesus I am more than a conqueror!"

"But thanks be to God! He gives us the victory through our
Lord Jesus Christ." **1 CORINTHIANS 15:57 (NIV 1984)**

LET THE SUN IN!

When you open the windows, do you have to beg the fresh air to come in? Or when you open the curtains in the morning, do you have to argue with the sun to make it shine into your room? How silly! You just open the windows and the air flows in. You open the curtains and the sun shines in.

The Bible says it's like that with God's peace. It will flow into our hearts, if we let it.

Are you worried? Are you anxious? Is anything troubling you today?

Don't try to work it all out by yourself. Let God's peace flow in—like sunshine into a dark room.

"Let the peace that comes from Christ rule in your hearts." COLOSSIANS 3:15 (NLT)

THE HORSE

Have you ever made something so beautiful you just had to run and show someone?

God is like that about everything he has made. He can't wait to show us.

Take the horse, God says—see how strong he is, and how proud, and what a beautiful mane he has, and how he can leap.

And just watch him gallop! And look how he loves to win races. I made that!

God loves the horse! He is so proud and thrilled with the horse that he wants to show him off to us.

If he loves the horse—how much more must he love you?

"I praise you, for I am fearfully and wonderfully made."
PSALM 139:14 (ESV)

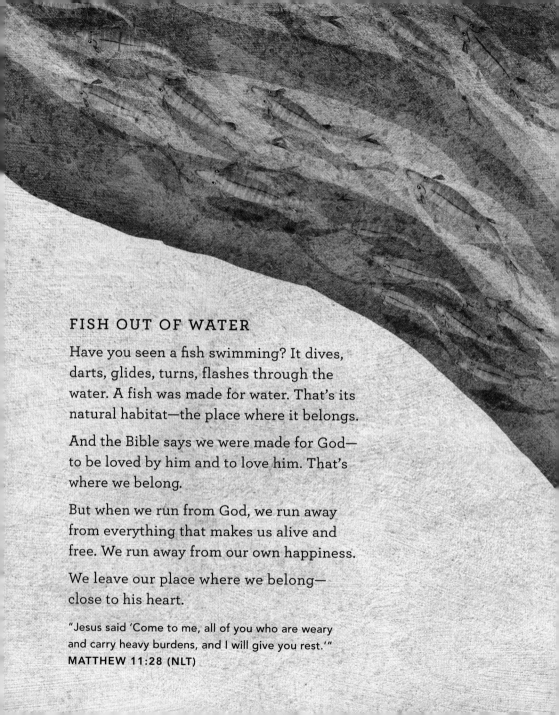

FISH OUT OF WATER

Have you seen a fish swimming? It dives, darts, glides, turns, flashes through the water. A fish was made for water. That's its natural habitat—the place where it belongs.

And the Bible says we were made for God— to be loved by him and to love him. That's where we belong.

But when we run from God, we run away from everything that makes us alive and free. We run away from our own happiness.

We leave our place where we belong— close to his heart.

"Jesus said 'Come to me, all of you who are weary and carry heavy burdens, and I will give you rest.'"
MATTHEW 11:28 (NLT)

FOOLISH FISH!

What if a fish one day decided, "I've had enough of being told what I can and can't do and only being allowed in water. I want to be FREE! I'm going to find my fortune on land!" and then jumped out of the water and onto the riverbank?

How far do you think that foolish fish would get?

It would wriggle and flap its fins, but of course fins don't work on land. It would lie there gasping for air and pretty soon it would die.

How free is that fish on land?

Not very.

The fish is not built for land.

And we are not built to be away from our Heavenly Father.

"So if the Son sets you free, you are truly free."
JOHN 8:36 (NLT)

GOOD NEWS!

In medieval times, do you know how you got your good news? A herald blew a trumpet. The herald would blow the trumpet to let you know "The battle is won!"

Good news is telling you something great has happened—something so wonderful that when you hear it, it fills your heart up with joy.

The Bible calls the true stories about Jesus's life "Good News like a herald would send."

Why are they Good News? Because they're telling us what Jesus has done to bring us home to God. They're telling us our Rescuer has come! And the battle is won!

"I bring you good news that will bring great joy to all people. The Savior ... has been born!"
LUKE 2:10, 11 (NLT)

NO BIRDS' NESTS!

Sometimes bad thoughts just land in your head from nowhere. Is having an awful thought a sin?

When Jesus was tempted in the desert, Satan whispered awful thoughts and lies to Jesus to tempt him away from God.

It's not the thoughts that count; it's what we do with those thoughts. Jesus didn't listen to those awful thoughts. He didn't believe them. He sent them away.

An old proverb says, "You can't help it if birds come and land on your head. But you don't have to let them build nests in your hair!"

"We take captive every thought to make it obedient to Christ." **2 CORINTHIANS 10:5 (NIV)**

GOD'S TITLE

When someone important is being introduced, the announcer usually says, "Mr. So-And-So—Founder of This Extra-Important Company!" or, "Miss Something Else—Nobel-Prize-Winning Inventor of This Brilliant Thing!"

Do you know how God likes to be introduced?

"His name is the Lord ... Father to the fatherless, defender of widows." **PSALM 68:4, 5 (NLT)**

Our Almighty God, who sifted stars through his fingers, stands not with kings and princes, but with the weak, the powerless, the poor.

Because the people no one else thinks are important have a special place in God's heart. He hears their cries. He fights for them and defends them.

And one night long ago, in Bethlehem, he stepped out of heaven and became one of them.

ARE WE TROUBLING GOD?

Do you sometimes think you can't bother God? That maybe he's too busy to hear from you? That what you're asking is too small to trouble him with?

Jesus said God wants us to come to him, like a child comes to her daddy. When we're afraid. When we're worried. If we're happy. If we're sad. However we feel. It doesn't matter. He wants us to come to him for everything.

Some people think God doesn't like to be troubled with us asking him things all the time.

But do you know the way to trouble him?

By not coming at all.

"Then you will call, and the Lord will answer;
you will cry for help, and he will say, 'Here I am.'"
ISAIAH 58:9 (NIV)

LIFTOFF!

What does a rocket need to lift off and go zooming into outer space? It needs a launchpad.

Do you know what God's launchpad is in our lives—from which he can do ANYTHING?

Is it great faith? Our perfect record?

Incredible courage?

No.

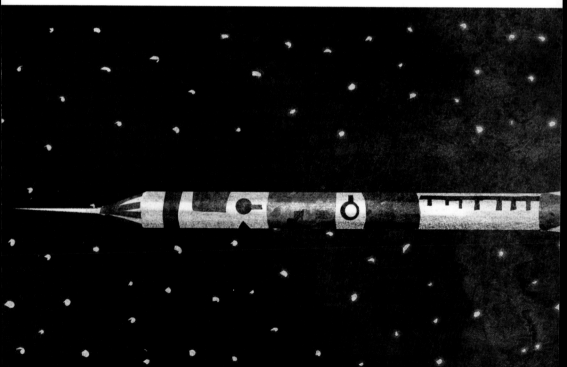

It's our weakness.

God's power comes to us in our littleness, in our brokenness, in our not knowing, in our not being able.

And when God's power meets our weakness?

Liftoff!

"My grace is all you need.
My power works best in weakness."
2 CORINTHIANS 12:9 (NLT)

RESTING AND RELYING

When you were little, did someone big ever carry you? Did you rest your head on his shoulder, lean your whole weight on him?

Faith is leaning your whole weight on God. Resting your head on his shoulder.

Faith means resting—relying—not on who we are, or what we can do, or how we feel, or what we know.

Faith is resting in who God is and what he has done.

And he has done EVERYTHING.

"And so we know and rely on the love God has for us."
1 JOHN 4:16 (NIV)

JUST BECAUSE!

When you're thinking up a reason, do you ever say, "Just Because"?

God says, "I love you—Just Because!"

He doesn't say, "I love you because you're kind" or, "I love you because you're helpful" or, "I love you because you're getting good grades" or even, "I love you because you love me."

God says, "The reason I love you is— I LOVE you!"

If God loved you because you're kind, that means if you stopped being kind, he'd stop loving you. Or if he loved you because you loved him, what if you stopped loving him?

God loves us—Just Because!

"Our God did not love us or choose us for anything in us; it was simply because he loves us."
DEUTERONOMY 7:7, 8 *(paraphrase)*

LIFE RAFT

Does it ever seem to you that nothing
in your life is right?

When things go wrong, God knows we
might start to wonder, Does God care
about me? Can he do anything about it
anyway?

So God makes you this promise to hold on
to—a life raft for his children in a storm:

> I am not hurting you.
> I have a Good Plan for you and
> a Bright Future for you.
> I am planning unending good
> for you in your life!

Things are not always as they seem.

But God is always up to something big.
Always up to something good.

"'For I know the plans I have for you,' declares
the Lord, 'plans to prosper you and not to harm
you, plans to give you hope and a future.'"
JEREMIAH 29:11 (NIV)

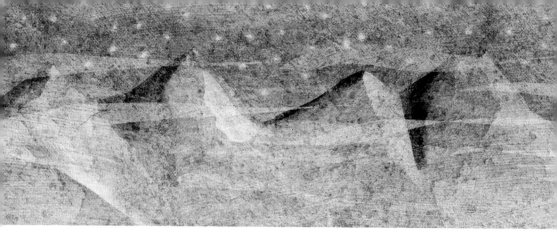

CLOUDS AND MOUNTAINS AND STARS

Have you noticed that when it's cloudy you can't see the stars? And that sometimes clouds can hide even mountains from you?

For a moment it seems as if there are no stars shining, no mountains standing.

Have the mountains moved? Have the stars stopped shining?

No. The clouds have just hidden them.

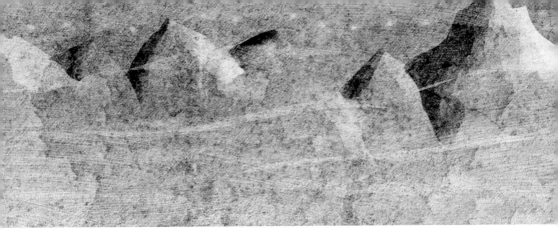

Feelings can be like clouds—they blow in and hide things from us. Sometimes they tell us God doesn't care. Or that God is far away.

The writer Amy Carmichael said, "Our feelings do not affect God's facts."

Our feelings come and go. But God stays the same. His promises still are shining.

"God is greater than our feelings." 1 JOHN 3:20 (NLT)

ACORN POWER

An acorn is only small. To look at it you'd think it was weak and not very important at all.

But from one acorn a mighty oak tree can grow.

And from one mighty oak tree a whole forest can grow!

A whole forest is inside a single acorn. And the Bible says because of Jesus all the riches of God—all of heaven's vast resources, all the power in the universe—have come to live inside you.

"You will be strengthened with all [God's] glorious power." **COLOSSIANS 1:11 (NLT)**

ALREADY ... BUT NOT YET!

We are living in between Already and Not Yet.

Jesus has ALREADY rescued us from the punishment of sin. We are forgiven and free!

But the world is still broken. We still sin. We still die. Things still aren't the way they are meant to be.

One day—but NOT YET—Jesus is coming back again. Not as a baby this time, but as King of the whole world. And then he will mend his broken world. There will be no more tears, or sickness, or dying. Even the trees will sing for joy!

While we wait, God wants us to remember: sin, sickness, tears, death—they won't last. They will come to an end.

But joy, love, life, and you—those are FOREVER.

"The night is nearly over; the day is almost here."
ROMANS 13:12 (NIV)

LIONS AND LAMBS

The Bible says that one day, at the end of time, when God comes back and makes his world the way it was always meant to be, lions will lie down with lambs.

Wait. That's impossible. A lion would eat a lamb!

But God says when he makes the world our perfect home again, even things that are impossible will come true.

God is making all the sad things come untrue. He is making the ending of the world happy. And all the dreams we have ever dreamed for ourselves? They are only shadows of the magnificent dreams God has dreamed for his children.

"All creation is waiting eagerly for that future day."
ROMANS 8:19 (NLT)

HOPE

When we use the word "hope," we say things like, "I hope we win!" It's like wishing for something we're not sure will happen.

But in the Bible, hope means being absolutely certain something will happen.

Jonathan Edwards, a preacher, said there are three things we can hope in if we belong to Jesus:

1. God will turn even the bad things around for your good in the end.
2. Your good things can't ever be taken away from you.
3. The best things are yet to come.

It doesn't mean that everything in our story is happy today. But that God is making the story end happily for the world—and for his children.

"The God of hope fill you with all joy and peace as you trust in him, so that you may overflow with hope ..."
ROMANS 15:13 (NIV)

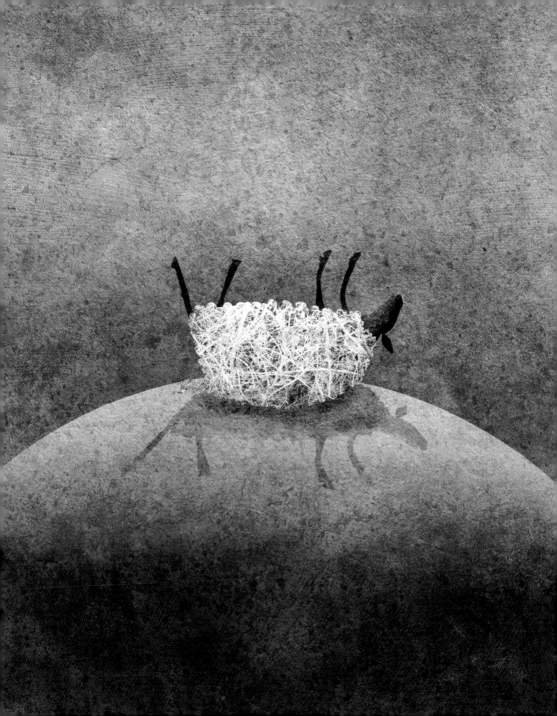

HELPLESS

What animal does the Bible say—four hundred times!—that people are most like?

Oh dear. It's sheep.

Sheep aren't clever at all. They're foolish.

For instance, sometimes they just topple over and can't get themselves back up again. They just lie there!

And they're constantly falling off cliffs. Or going to unsafe places and getting stuck. Or eating poisonous things. Or getting hurt. Or running off and getting lost. Or not finding their way home again—even if their fold is in plain sight!

So you see, sheep are completely helpless on their own and desperately need a shepherd.

And God says we are helpless on our own too. And we desperately need a Shepherd.

Which is why he gave us Jesus.

"He tends his flock like a shepherd: He gathers the lambs in his arms." ISAIAH 40:11 (NIV)

CLOSE TO HIS HEART

Even when the shepherd finds his lost sheep
it goes rushing all about—and the only way
he can round it up is to seize it, hurl it to
the ground, bind its legs, and throw it over
his shoulders and carry it home.

The poor sheep doesn't understand. It
thinks it's being captured—killed!

But the shepherd is saving its life.

And sometimes we don't understand what
God is doing in our lives either. It may
even look like God is hurting you.

But you can trust your Shepherd, who loves
you. He carries you close to his heart.

"He will carry the lambs in his arms, holding them close
to his heart." ISAIAH 40:11 (NLT)

GOOD SHEPHERD

[Jesus said,] "I am the good shepherd
… I sacrifice my life for the sheep."
JOHN 10:14, 15 (NLT)

Don't be afraid, Little Flock,
I'm your Good Shepherd.
You have everything you need.

When you're hungry,
I'll feed you.

When you're thirsty,
I'll give you water to drink.

When you're tired,
I'll bring you to cool shade
where you can rest.

I will rescue you.

Protect you.

Love you.

GETTING FOUND

Now, if you think a sheep is hopeless about finding its way home, what about a coin?

Jesus told a story of a woman who lost a coin and turned her entire house upside down to find it.

Can the coin do something to be found? Can it get up and search for its owner? How silly!

The Bible says we are as helpless as a coin that is lost. If we find God, it's because he found us first. It's because he opened up our hearts to him so we could believe in him.

Because it's not about us doing something to find God.

It's about God who did everything to find us!

"We love because he first loved us."
1 JOHN 4:19 (NIV)

ARROW PRAYERS

Do you think that maybe your prayers aren't long enough? Or don't use enough special words?

In the Bible there are lots of little prayers— so little they couldn't be any littler. "Help, Lord!", "Lord, save me!" They're arrow prayers, quickly shot up to God.

Once, in the middle of the night, during a huge storm, Jesus came to see his friends on the lake—walking on top of the water. Peter wanted to try, so Jesus said, "Come on!"

Peter stepped out of the boat and walked on water. But then he looked down—and, starting to sink, cried, "Lord, save me!" Immediately, Jesus caught him.

Your prayer might be so little that it may not seem like a prayer at all.

But it's enough. God hears it.

"'Save me, Lord!' he shouted."
MATTHEW 14:30–31 (NLT)

TO MAKE YOUR HEART SING!

There's not a single thing in this universe—no star, no mountain, no puppy, no flower—that wasn't planned, designed, and given to us by God. And meant by God to do one thing.

What?

To make your heart sing!

The preacher John Calvin said: "There is not one blade of grass, there is no color in this world that is not intended to make us rejoice."

"We will sing for joy to the end of our lives." **PSALM 90:14** (paraphrase)

DYING, WAKING

God meant us to live forever. But sin
has broken everything and now we—
all of us—die.

Jesus came to destroy death. He died on
the cross and was buried—but death
couldn't keep him dead. On the third
day he burst out of the tomb!

And now death can't keep us dead either.

The preacher Charles Spurgeon said
that Jesus has turned the tomb into a bed—
and dying into just waking up.

We will still die. But after we die, we will
wake—as if from a refreshing night's
sleep—and Jesus will lead us by the hand
into Life that won't ever end.

[Jesus said,] "Anyone who believes in me will live,
even after dying." JOHN 11:25 (NLT)

WHALES, OCEANS, AND YOU

The deep, dark, rolling oceans are vast and mighty! So deep even sunlight can't reach down to the bottom of the ocean floor.

So immense that they cover nearly three quarters of the earth's surface!

And the Bible says God holds them in the palm of his hand.

If he can hold the oceans in the hollow of his hand, he can hold you.

"In his hand are the depths of the earth, and the mountain peaks belong to him." **PSALM 95:4 (NIV)**

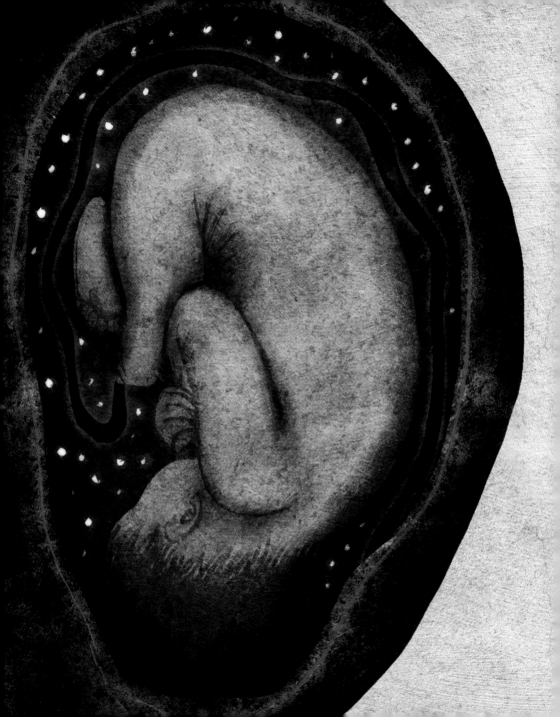

ON PURPOSE

Did you just end up here on earth? Was it all an accident?

The Bible says it wasn't a mistake or an accident. It was a plan.

You didn't just end up here. God put you here on purpose.

God wanted you here, and he had to have you here right now. Because he has a wonderful plan for you—something that only you can do.

Every single thing about you—the color of your eyes, your name, what you love, every day you will live—God knew before time began.

Even before you were born, he loved you. You began in God's heart.

You are his. Made by him. Made for him.

"You saw my body as it was formed. All the days planned for me ... before I was one day old."
PSALM 139:16 (NCV)

WHO ARE YOU?

When you first meet someone, she might ask, "Who are you?"

And you might say, "Well I'm So-and-So. And I am very good at this thing and that thing and here's where I live and this is my family and—"

But do you know who God says you are?

The one Jesus loves.

"The Son of God ... loved me and gave himself for me."
GALATIANS 2:20 (KJV)

POOR QUASIMODO!

Do you think you're not good enough for Jesus to love you?

Victor Hugo wrote a story called *The Hunchback of Notre Dame*. It's about Quasimodo, who is so ugly he hides up in the bell tower. He is afraid that anyone who sees him will be disgusted.

But we don't have to be like poor Quasimodo.

Jesus came to bring you out of the shadows. He sees you and he loves you—just as you are, not as you should be.

Let him love you—just as you are.

"You are the God who sees me." **GENESIS 16:13 (NIV)**

MISSING SHOVEL

In World War II, prisoners of war were building a railroad. After their day's work, the shovels were counted. The guard became enraged. One was missing.

The prisoners were lined up and ordered to stand there until someone admitted they'd stolen the shovel. No one said it was them. The guard shouted. Still no one budged. The guard threatened to kill all of them unless someone owned up.

At last one man stepped forward and said he had done it. The guard killed him.

Later, at the guardhouse, the tools were recounted. No shovel was missing.

The innocent man had sacrificed his life to save the others.

Two thousand years ago an innocent man stepped forward for us and sacrificed his life to save us.

"There is no greater love than to lay down one's life for one's friends." **JOHN 15:13 (NLT)**

REDEEMED!

The Bible says sin is in charge of us—and we are its slaves. Sin is keeping us from being all we could be in every area of our lives. It has robbed us of our freedom and our hearts are in chains.

How do slaves get free? Someone "redeems" them—pays the price to buy them back out of slavery and set them free.

The Bible says Jesus redeemed us out of slavery to sin. How?

He paid the price to get us back.

What was the price?

His life.

"The Son of Man came ... to give his life as a ransom for many." MARK 10:45 (NLT)

FREED!

We were slaves to sin. But Jesus paid the price to buy our freedom. And now we're free! Wait. Free to do whatever we like?

There is a story from the American Civil War of a Northerner who bought a young slave girl at a slave auction. As they left the auction, the man turned to the girl and said, "You're free!"

She turned to him in amazement. "You mean I'm free to do whatever I want?"

"Yes," he said.

"And to say whatever I want to say?"

"Yes, anything."

"And to be whatever I want to be?"

"Yes!"

"And even go wherever I want to go?"

"Yes!" He laughed. "You're free to go wherever you'd like!"

She looked at him intently and replied, "Then I will go with you."

[Jesus said,] "I no longer call you slaves ... Now you are my friends." **JOHN 15:15 (NLT)**

after Piero Della Francesco

FINISHED!

Just before he died, Jesus shouted from the cross, "It is finished!"

What was finished?

Jesus was saying:

> Everything you need to come back home to God,
>
> Everything you need to be free and happy in God,
>
> Everything you need to live forever, I've done it all!

It wasn't a cry of defeat. It was a shout of victory. The great work of rescuing us was finished!

There is now nothing you can do to make God love you more—and nothing you can do to make him love you less.

It is finished!

"Thanks be to God for his indescribable gift!"
2 CORINTHIANS 9:15 (NIV)

TOPSY-TURVY

The true story of God coming to rescue his children is Topsy-Turvy Good News!

Jesus said, "The way to be the greatest is to be the least. The way to save your life is to give it away."

Jesus didn't come with wealth. He came as a poor man.

He didn't come as a General to grab power. He came as a baby.

He didn't come to be Boss of everyone. He came to be a servant.

And—without fighting a single military battle—God's Undercover Prince conquered the whole world!

"But God chose ... the weak things of the world to shame the strong." **1 CORINTHIANS 1:27 (NCV)**

CHANGED!

How can I come to God?—someone is saying—I've been too bad!

Remember those Great Heroes in the Bible—Moses, King David, and Saint Paul? Guess what they all had in common.

Big beards? Well, yes. (After all, it was Bible times.) But what else?

They were always good? No.

They were courageous? No.

They were all—every last one of them—murderers.

If God can transform such terrible sinners—if he can take Moses and turn him into a great leader, if he can take David and turn him into a great king, if he can take Paul and turn him into a great preacher—what might he do with you?

[Jesus answered,] "I have come to call ... those who know they are sinners and need to repent."
LUKE 5:32 (NLT)

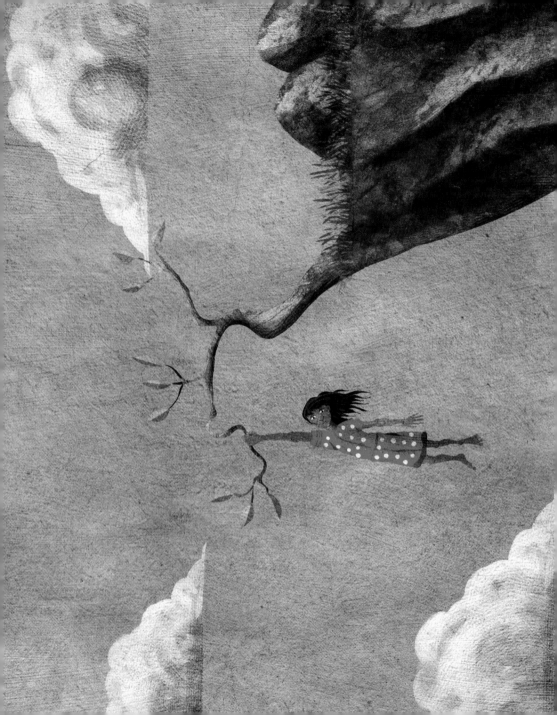

BELIEVING AND DOUBTING

But, someone is saying, What if I can't believe enough?

Imagine you're on a hike up a big mountain and you lose your foothold. Just before you plunge over the precipice, you spot a branch.

Do you need to believe in that branch for it to save you? You don't worry about that— you just grab it!

Faith is like grabbing on to that branch. We just reach out for God. And he is the one who saves us.

Our strong God is the one who rescues us— not our strong faith.

Because faith isn't just you holding on to God. It's God holding on to you.

"I do believe, but help me overcome my unbelief!"
MARK 9:24 (NLT)

TRYING AND TRUSTING

A preacher called David Martyn Lloyd-Jones sometimes asked people, "Are you a Christian?"

If they said, "I'm trying!" he knew they didn't really understand. Because being a Christian isn't about trying. It's about trusting.

Trusting not in what you must do. But in what God has done.

And he has done EVERYTHING!

"But to all who believed [in Jesus] and accepted him, he gave the right to become children of God."
JOHN 1:12 (NLT)

DON'T BE A DONKEY!

Wild donkeys hate to be led. They run away if you go anywhere near them and won't come unless you force them with bridles and bits. All they want is to be away from you and do whatever they like!

God doesn't want his children to be like donkeys—always fighting him and running away.

Being close to God is what we were made for.

God sent his only Son to draw near to us. It cost him everything to love us.

So don't be a donkey—that needs a bridle and a bit to come near. Let God love you. Teach you. Lead you.

He knows the way.

"Don't be like a horse or donkey, that doesn't understand. They must be led with bits and reins, or they will not come near you." PSALM 32:9 (NCV)

GOD'S PRESCRIPTION

Do you have any problems today? Did you know God has a Prescription for problems?

Corrie ten Boom, who was sent to a concentration camp for saving Jews in World War II, wrote, "Let God's promises shine on your problems."

What has God promised us?

> To be with us.
> Always to love us.
> To guard our hearts with peace,
> like a sentry.
> To go ahead of us and lead us.
> To follow behind us and protect us.
> To walk beside us and be our friend.

Perhaps that's our only real problem—forgetting just how great our God is!

"All the Lord's promises prove true."
PSALM 18:30 (NLT)

ALL! EVERYTHING! ALWAYS!

God told Moses to go and see Pharaoh. But Moses was too shy and had a stutter and didn't think he could. Do you ever feel like that? That you can't do what God asks you to do?

Wait. Whoever said anything about what you can do?

God turned Moses into a great leader and through him changed the world!

Are you worrying about anything today? Does something seem too big for you? Then God makes you his All-Everything-Always Promise:

"All the time, in everything,
I am always sending you everything you need
so you can always do all I ever ask you to!"
2 CORINTHIANS 9:8 *(paraphrase)*

It doesn't matter who you are or what you can do.

It matters who God is and what he can do.

And he can do ANYTHING!

BUT WE MISS OUR ONIONS!

God's people were slaves in Egypt. So God rescued them.

God had divided the sea. He'd moved a cloud. He'd sent a pillar of fire. He'd given them water from a rock and rained down bread from heaven.

And still his people didn't trust him. "God hates us!" they said.

God had saved their lives and they said, "But we miss our onions!"

Sometimes we're like those ungrateful people grumbling in their tents about onions. That's what sin is—not seeing that every single thing we have is a gift from God. It's why God tells us to be always thanking him.

Why does he need us to thank him?

He doesn't. But we do.

You see, God knows it will fill our hearts with joy.

"Give thanks to the Lord, for he is good!"
1 CHRONICLES 16:34 (NLT)

WHY WORRY?

Worry is thinking we know better than
God how something should go.

Jesus said God doesn't want his children
to worry—and then told us to watch the
little birds and let them be our teachers.

> "Said the Robin to the Sparrow,
> 'I should really like to know
> Why these anxious human beings
> Rush about and hurry so.'

> "Said the Sparrow to the Robin,
> 'Friend, I think that it must be
> That they have no Heavenly Father
> Such as cares for you and me.'"

> —Elizabeth Cheney, 1859

"Do not worry about your life, what you will eat or
drink ... Look at the birds of the air; they do not sow
or reap or store away in barns, and yet your heavenly
Father feeds them." MATTHEW 6:25–26 (NIV)

GRAINS OF SAND

Have you ever been so excited about something you can't stop thinking about it?

Do you know what the Bible says?
God can't stop thinking about you.

If you tried to count how many times he thinks of you, you couldn't—it's more than all the grains of sand on the seashore!

And every single thought God has about you is always only about how he can do good for you. All day and all night he is thinking of ways to bless you, encourage you, strengthen you, help you.

With such a loving Heavenly Father, why ever would you be afraid?

"How precious are your thoughts about me, O God ...
I can't even count them; they outnumber the grains
of sand!" **PSALM 139:17–18 (NLT)**

COMFORTER

[Jesus said,] "I will pray the Father, and he shall give you another Comforter." **JOHN 14:16 (KJV)**

God's Spirit is called the "Comforter." Does it make you think of a nice comfy quilt—all cozy and warm?

Oh dear.

In the Bayeux tapestry of 1066, there's a knight on a horse and the caption reads: "Bishop Odo comforts his troops."

Is Bishop Odo giving them nice fluffy quilts? No. Look! He's prodding them from behind with a stick! NOT comfy.

But Odo is spurring them on, encouraging them, urging them to keep going and not give up. Because comfort in the Bible doesn't mean "to make comfy." It means "to send help."

When we want to give up, when we are afraid, God sends his spirit—the Comforter—to make us strong, to give us courage, to lift us up.

MIGHTY MAN OF VALOR!

"The angel ... said ..., 'The Lord is with you, O mighty man of valor.'" **JUDGES 6:12 (ESV)**

Who is this Fearsome Warrior the angel is talking to? See that puny weakling hiding over there in the wine press?

"He's the man for the job!" God said.

Gideon: the smallest son of the smallest family of the smallest tribe of Israel.
Why on earth would God choose him?
And call him "mighty" when he was nothing of the sort?

But God called Gideon by his true name, and Gideon became what God knew he was all along—MIGHTY!

Because God sees not just who you are— but who he is going to make you.

NAGGING GOD

Is it okay to nag God? And pester him?

God says we MUST!

God tells us to give him no rest, to remind him of what he has done and what he says he will do, and not to stop until he answers.

God loves it when we ask him for great things! Because he is a King—and Kings love to do marvelous, powerful things.

> "Thou art coming to a King,
>   Large petitions with thee bring;
>   For His grace and power are such,
>   None can ever ask too much ... "
> —John Newton

"Take no rest, all you who pray to the Lord. Give the Lord no rest." ISAIAH 62:6–7 (NLT)

MIRACULOUS WORLD!

A giraffe can clean its ear with its twenty-one-inch tongue! A hippo isn't yawning at you—it's showing off its teeth so birds will clean them. No two zebras have stripes exactly alike. Fifty thousand cells in your body will die and be replaced all while you read this sentence.

We live in an incredible, miraculous world!

The Bible says nature is just a shadow of what it will be when God comes back to mend his broken world.

If this beautiful world is just a shadow of what it will be like when God comes back … what on earth will you be like?

"The mountains and hills will burst into song, and the trees of the field will clap their hands!"
ISAIAH 55:12 (NLT)

THE YOUNG CHAMPION

"Jesus, the champion who ... because of the joy awaiting him ... endured the cross." **HEBREWS 12:2 (NLT)**

The Bible says life is like running a race—but only one person has ever run that race perfectly.

Jesus came to earth as a man and ran the race of life. Even though his heart broke—he never stopped. He kept on running. Even when it led to the cross.

Why? He was running for a Prize—for the Joy set before him.

What Prize? Jesus was God—he already had everything! What could he possibly need? What Joy did he not already have in heaven? That he had to come to earth to get? That he could only get by dying on the cross?

You.

You are Jesus's Prize. You are his Joy. You are what he came to win.

SMALL AND SCREECHY

If you had to pick one bird out of the nine thousand species in the world to talk about, which one would you pick? A Peacock? A Kingfisher? Someone Fancy?

Jesus chose the drabbest, dullest, commonest, brashest, most irritating, badly behaved, small, and screechy bird—one that doesn't even have its own song.

He chose the sparrow. And said every single sparrow is made by God, looked after by him and loved by him.

God, who made the endless galaxies and planets and the stars in the vast heavens, says a tiny sparrow doesn't come to the end of its tiny life without him noticing.

If God cares for the tiniest sparrow, how much more must he care for you, his child?

"Not a single sparrow can fall to the ground without your Father knowing it." MATTHEW 10:29 (NLT)

STAIRCASE FOR BOATS

When a riverboat needs to go up a hill, it navigates through a lock (which is basically a staircase for boats).

The boat enters a sealed chamber.

Gradually, the water level is raised, lifting the boat up, until the water inside is at the same level as the river ahead. The gates open and the boat continues on.

But from the boat entering the lock—you can't see the river ahead. It looks like a dead end!

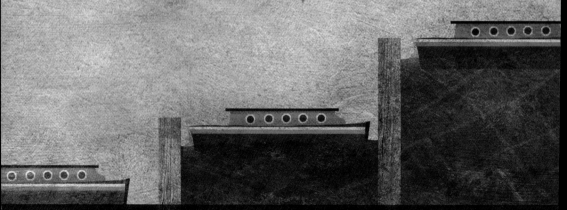

And the Bible says we can't see everything God is doing in our lives either. But what looks like a dead end is really God lifting you up.

Because there are no dead ends with God. Only new beginnings in disguise.

"God causes everything to work together for the good of those who love God." **ROMANS 8:28 (NLT)**

TRUE COLORS

Did you know that leaves aren't really green? They only seem that way.

Each leaf contains chlorophyll—the green color that captures light and turns it into food for the tree. It's this green that hides the leaf's true color. In the autumn, trees produce less chlorophyll, the green fades, and so the leaves show their true colors— blazing reds, yellows, golds!

The leaves were always those brilliant colors—we just couldn't see them.

And the Bible says you can't see all you really are either.

But one day, when God mends his broken world once and for all, you'll be all he made you to be—and then your true colors will come shining through.

"All creation is waiting eagerly for that future day when God will reveal who his children really are."
ROMANS 8:19 (NLT)

RADAR IN FOG

The only way pilots can fly in fog is by trusting their radar. Radar tells you about things that are there, but are too far away or too hidden for your eyes to see.

Corrie ten Boom said, "Faith is like radar that sees through fog."

Faith knows what is there and tells us—even when we can't actually see it with our eyes.

We can't see God with our eyes, but faith tells us he is there.

"Faith means being sure of the things we hope for and knowing that something is real even if we do not see it."
HEBREWS 11:1 (NCV)

UNDER HIS WINGS

Are you ever afraid? Do what baby chicks do!

At the first sign of danger—if there's a storm coming or a hawk hovering—a mother hen spreads out her wings and clucks to her babies, and they run straight under her feathers.

The mother draws her wings in tight, tucking every one of her little chicks safely under her. Nothing can touch those babies.

And we have a Heavenly Father who says he loves us and cares for us like that.

When we are afraid, he tells us to run to him. We can nestle up under his wings. And he will protect us.

"He will cover you with his feathers, and under his wings you will find refuge." **PSALM 91:3–4 (NIV)**

TALK TO YOURSELF!

Why are people usually unhappy?

David Martyn Lloyd-Jones said it's because people are listening to themselves instead of talking to themselves.

When you wake up in the morning, you can listen to whatever your thoughts are telling you—maybe they are reminding you of something bad you did the day before, maybe they are making you scared of something you have to do tomorrow. You can listen and feel horrible.

Or you can talk back. You can remind yourself of what is true, and who you are, and who God is and what he has done.

You can say something like:

"Why am I discouraged? Why is my heart so sad? I will put my hope in God!" **PSALM 42:11 (NLT)**

Are you listening to yourself today ... or talking to yourself?

SKYSCRAPER

Do you ever feel like nothing good is happening in your life?

When a skyscraper is built, what's the first thing the builders do? Dig a huge hole. Wait. They're going the wrong way! For years, the construction site is just a hole in the ground. It looks like nothing's happening.

But the builders would tell you they are laying the foundation—the part you don't see that keeps the tower from falling over. The higher they build, the deeper they must dig.

They are digging down to go up.

And the Bible says God will use even the bad things—which won't last—to do something good, to build something beautiful in us that will last forever.

He is digging down to go up.

"For our present troubles ... produce for us a glory that vastly outweighs them and will last forever!" **2 CORINTHIANS 4:17 (NLT)**

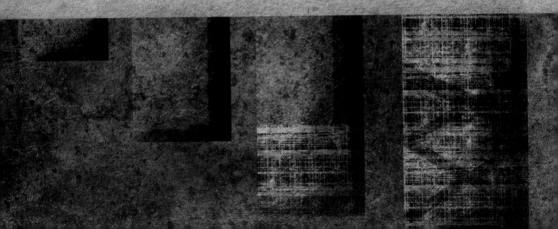

GOD'S BATTLE PLAN

King Jehoshaphat was alarmed.

Well, you can't blame him. Three countries had banded together and were marching against him. God's people were completely overpowered. What would Jehoshaphat do?

Send his mightiest fighting men? Send soldiers and swords and spears? No.

He sent a little choir.

Pardon?

And some songs.

Excuse me?

"Give thanks to the Lord!" they sang. "His love never ends!"

It so confused the other army that they started fighting each other, and by the time the choir reached the battlefield they found no more enemies left.

When God's children sing to him, it moves the heart of God and invites him into what's happening—and chases the enemy away.

Is anything overpowering you today?

You know what to do!

"Sing to him." **PSALM 105:2 (NIV)**

FLY YOUR FLAG!

How do you know when the king is in residence at his castle? The flag is flying over the castle. It tells everyone he's at home.

The Bible says when Jesus comes to live in your heart he brings his flag with him. It flies over your life, showing everyone the King is at home.

What is Jesus's Flag?

G. K. Chesterton called it "the gigantic secret of the Christian."

What is it?

Joy.

"Joy and gladness will be found in her, thanksgiving and the sound of singing." ISAIAH 51:3 (NIV)

GOD MATH

Do you know God Math? It's nothing like ours! For instance, according to God Math:

> 5 loaves + 2 fish = enough food
> to feed 5,000 (+ leftovers)

> 1 lost sheep = as valuable as 99

Gideon was the leader of God's army. But God told him, "Your army of 32,000 is way too large to defeat the Midianites." Too large? Wait. What?

Twice, God had Gideon actually reduce his army—until it was small enough to win the battle. Small enough?

God would give Gideon's army the victory, but he wanted them to rely on him and not their own strength.

Gideon's army of 300 was outnumbered— 450 to one! But remember God Math?

> God + nothing = everything.

> Everything - God = nothing.

"'It is not by force nor by strength, but by my Spirit,' says the Lord." **ZECHARIAH 4:6 (NLT)**

TODAY

Every morning we enter a new day. Who knows what the day will bring?

God knows.

Which is why he tells us not to be afraid. He has already gone ahead of us into the new day. He knows the way, what will happen, all we'll need.

In the morning we can put our day in his hands. And let him bring into our day whatever he has for us.

And then, in the evening, we give it back to him. And trust him with all that happened in it.

"Do not be afraid or discouraged, for the Lord will personally go ahead of you. He will be with you." **DEUTERONOMY 31:8 (NLT)**

GOD'S PHONE NUMBER

Do you know God's phone number?

It's Jeremiah–333.

You can call it any time. His line is never busy. It won't ever go to voice mail. He'll always pick up.

In fact, God says he is waiting for your call. He wants you to call to him because he has wonderful things he wants to tell you.

He longs to hear the sound of your voice. Day after day, he is waiting.

So call him—Jeremiah 33:3!

He can't wait to tell you wonderful things.

"Call to me and I will answer you and tell you great and unsearchable things you do not know."
JEREMIAH 33:3 (NIV)

DON'T BE AFRAID!

Whenever God talks to his children in the Bible, do you know what he usually says first?

"Hello"? "How do you do"?

No. He says, "Don't be afraid!"

God must not want his children—even for a moment—living anxiously or afraid. He wants his children to trust him.

Are you worried about something today? Is something frightening you?

God says to you, "Don't be afraid. I am with you. I will help you."

Whatever it is, you can put it in God's hands.

"But Jesus spoke to them at once. 'Don't be afraid,' he said. 'Take courage. I am here!'" **MATTHEW 14:27 (NLT)**

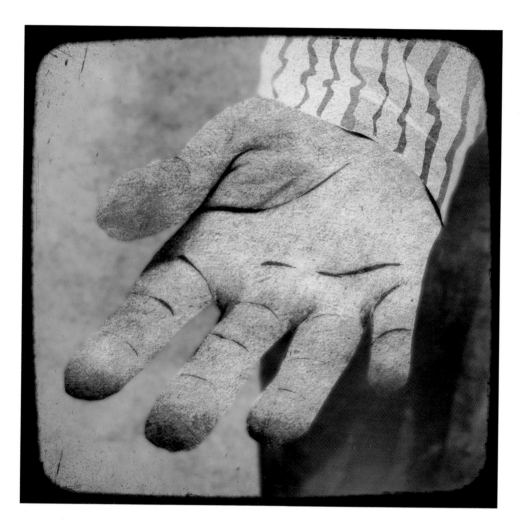

WILD AND DANGEROUS

What's the hardest thing in the world to tame? A lion?

Here's a clue—it's tiny.

An ant? No. The Bible says this thing is so dangerous it can set a forest on fire. It's also the strongest part of the human body.

The leg? No. It's right under your nose.

The tongue.

It's small, but the Bible says the tongue is like a rudder on a great boat. It can steer your whole life. What we say leads us where we go. Our words can do terrible damage. They hurt people. And we can't ever unsay them.

What can we do?

Jesus is called the Word of Life—because when he speaks, life happens.

Listen to him. He will heal your heart— and your words.

"Take control of what I say, O Lord, and guard my lips."
PSALM 141:3 (NLT)

STILLED STORM

One night, Jesus and his helpers were going out for a nice, quiet sail in their little boat ... Out of nowhere, hurricane-force winds hit the lake, whipping the water up into towering, churning, surging waves. Jesus's friends thought they were going to drown!

But Jesus spoke to the storm. "Quiet," he said. "Be still." And the storm stopped.

Do you ever feel anxious in your heart?

If Jesus can calm a storm on a lake, he can calm the storm in your heart.

"Give all your worries and cares to God, for he cares about you." **1 PETER 5:7 (NLT)**

SUPERPOWER STRENGTH

"… the incredible greatness of God's power for us who believe him." **EPHESIANS 1:19 (NLT)**

God's power is incomparable! Immeasurable! Unimaginable! How do you fit it inside words?

A writer in the Bible tried. Paul used three Greek words to describe it—"hyperballo," "megathos," and "dynamis." Basically, "Hyper-Mega-Dynamite!"

But there's more. Paul says this power is FOR YOU.

You don't have to do everything by yourself. You don't have to be strong enough or brave enough to face things alone. Because God has given you his superpower strength!

HAPPY BIRTHDAY!

The Queen of England has two birthdays. On her official birthday she has to do Queen Things. But on her actual birthday she gets to do whatever she fancies (like eat ice cream in her slippers all day if she wants).

Wouldn't you like two birthdays? Actually, when you belong to Jesus, you have THREE birthdays!

There's your birthday when you were born into the world as a baby.

Then there's your birthday when you say yes to Jesus and you are born all over again into God's whole new life.

And then there's the birthday after you die— when Jesus takes you by the hand and leads you through death—and you wake up with him into Perfect Life that won't ever end.

"You have been born again, but ... [y]our new life will last forever." **1 PETER 1:23 (NLT)**

LEAP INTO LIGHT!

Faith is believing what God says.

Some people think faith is like taking a leap in the dark, that faith is blind.

But the Bible says it's the opposite. Away from God we are in the dark. That's when we are blind, stumbling around.

John Newton was a notorious slave trader—but coming to know Jesus changed him forever. He spent the rest of his life working to free slaves and wrote the hymn "Amazing Grace": "I once was blind," he sang, "but now I see!"

When we come home to God it is not a leap into darkness.

It is a magnificent leap into light—the light of God's love for us!

"Jesus [said], 'I am the light of the world: he that followeth me shall not walk in darkness, but shall have the light of life.'" JOHN 8:12 (KJV)

FORGIVEN!

"Forgive each other just as God forgave you in Christ."
EPHESIANS 4:32 (NCV)

God tells us to forgive others. But, you say, how can I forgive them when what they did was wrong?

How can we forgive? We can't. Not by ourselves.

The only way is if Jesus's love fills up our hearts. When we think of Jesus dying for us, loving us, forgiving us—when we didn't deserve it—how can we not forgive others?

Jesus will help you do what you cannot do.

The strange thing is, we may think if we forgive someone we're letting them off— just letting them go free!

But do you know? It's exactly the other way around.

When you forgive, you do let someone go free—you set a prisoner free! But that prisoner is you.

THE LITTLE BIRD TEACHERS

"Ask the birds of the sky, and they will tell you." **JOB 12:7 (NLT)**

Did you know God wants us to be bird watchers? He says to us:

> Look at the sparrows: they are not very important and yet I love them and know all about them. How much more must I love you?

> Look at the ravens: they don't sow or reap. They have no barns or pantries. Yet I feed them. How much more will I look after you?

> Look at the storks: they go away but they always come home. Be always coming home to me!

> Be like the little birds who know their Heavenly Father loves them and will take care of them.

> Be like the birds who look to me for what they need at the proper time—look to me for EVERYTHING!

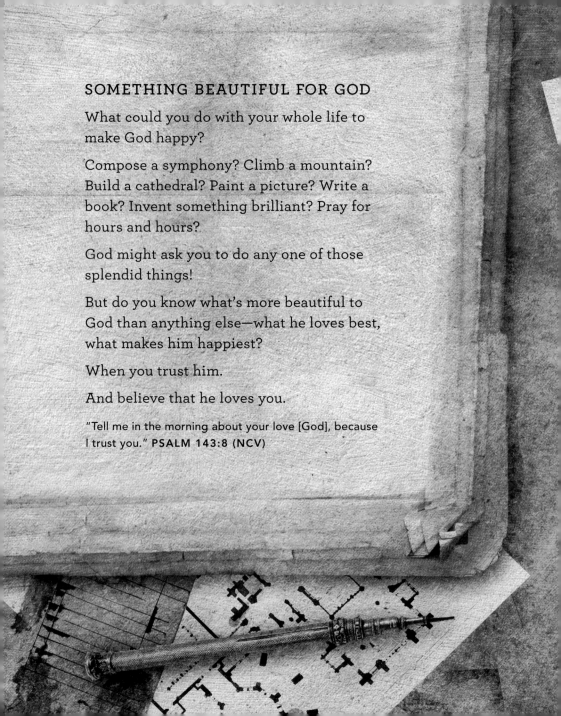

SOMETHING BEAUTIFUL FOR GOD

What could you do with your whole life to make God happy?

Compose a symphony? Climb a mountain? Build a cathedral? Paint a picture? Write a book? Invent something brilliant? Pray for hours and hours?

God might ask you to do any one of those splendid things!

But do you know what's more beautiful to God than anything else—what he loves best, what makes him happiest?

When you trust him.

And believe that he loves you.

"Tell me in the morning about your love [God], because I trust you." **PSALM 143:8 (NCV)**

LIKE A DEER

High, steep, rocky, craggy, scary places—a deer's feet are made for places like this. Deer can stand on the highest places in the world.

The Bible says God has some high places for you as well. The path God takes you on may be steep. The climb may be hard. The trail may be narrow. The way might be perilous. But he has promised to be with you. He will always make sure there is a perfect way for you to go through.

He makes you as sure-footed as a deer—made for the heights.

"God . . . makes my way perfect. He makes me as surefooted as a deer, enabling me to stand on mountain heights."
PSALM 18:32–33 (NLT)

BELIEVE

"God is able to do whatever he promises." **ROMANS 4:21 (NLT)**

God asked Noah to build a boat in the middle
of a desert—when there wasn't a single cloud in
the sky! Abraham was one hundred, his wife was
ninety—and God promised them a baby! God
told Joshua to defeat the city of Jericho not by
fighting—but by shouting!

Sound crazy? Sometimes God asks his children to do things they don't understand. And he promises to do things people say are impossible.

Who will you believe?

What your eyes can see? What your mind can imagine?

Or what God tells you?

GOD'S GALLERY

God made all things—just for the joy of it. Like an artist.

Jonathan Edwards said the whole world is like God's gallery—displaying God's magnificent works of art. Everything around us is telling us about God.

Every snowflake whispers, "It's God who made us beautiful—not us, but him!"

Every woodland creature proclaims, "How beautiful is the one who made us!"

God is singing to our hearts through a silver birch blazing like lightning in a forest of firs.

The universe is telling us it didn't create itself.

God did!

And do you know what God says is his absolute Masterpiece?

You.

"For we are God's masterpiece." EPHESIANS 2:10 (NLT)

KNOWING GOD

God's world is shining all around us. The skies, streams, trees, animals—without needing any words at all—are telling us God is powerful and wise and beautiful.

But they can't tell us everything. They can't tell us the most important thing.

They can't tell us about his love. His Wonderful Never Stopping, Never Giving Up, Unbreaking, Always and Forever Love!

The love that made the stars. That moved heaven and earth to be near us. That came down to live with us.

No. To really see God's love, we must look at Jesus.

"Christ is the visible image of the invisible God."
COLOSSIANS 1:15 (NLT)

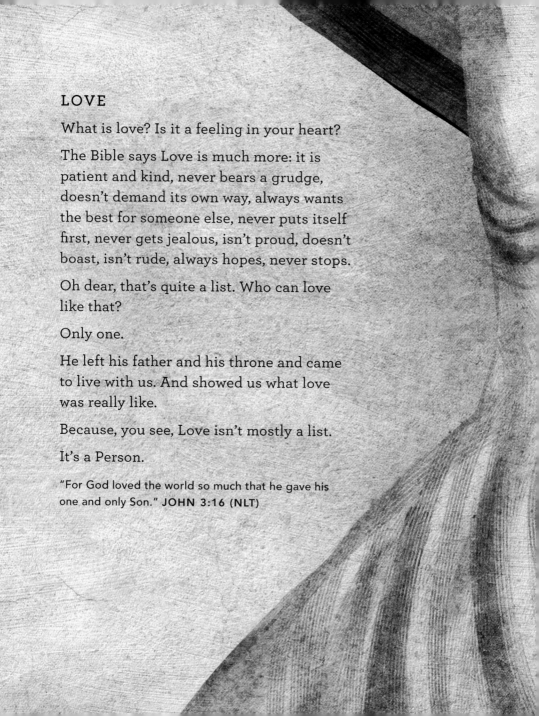

LOVE

What is love? Is it a feeling in your heart?

The Bible says Love is much more: it is patient and kind, never bears a grudge, doesn't demand its own way, always wants the best for someone else, never puts itself first, never gets jealous, isn't proud, doesn't boast, isn't rude, always hopes, never stops.

Oh dear, that's quite a list. Who can love like that?

Only one.

He left his father and his throne and came to live with us. And showed us what love was really like.

Because, you see, Love isn't mostly a list.

It's a Person.

"For God loved the world so much that he gave his one and only Son." **JOHN 3:16 (NLT)**

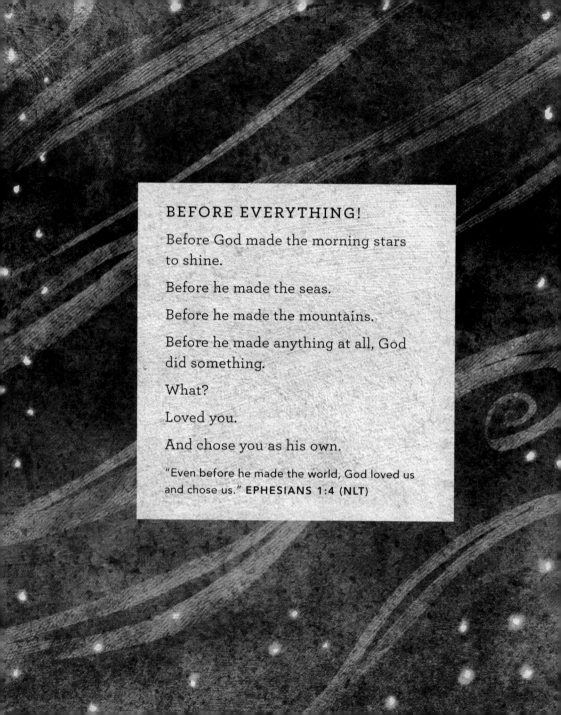

BEFORE EVERYTHING!

Before God made the morning stars to shine.

Before he made the seas.

Before he made the mountains.

Before he made anything at all, God did something.

What?

Loved you.

And chose you as his own.

"Even before he made the world, God loved us and chose us." **EPHESIANS 1:4 (NLT)**

BUT GOD!

Those two little words are the most important in the whole Bible—they show up 3,930 times.

When everything looks like it's over, when there's no hope—But God! God does something. He turns it all around. Those words are like a fire engine rounding the bend. Help is on the way!

Adam and Eve left the garden. "**But God** whispered a promise to them."

A flood was coming. "**But God** remembered Noah."

We were helpless. "**But God** showed his great love for us by sending Christ."

Whatever is happening in your life today— look up! Help is on the way.

"My flesh and my heart may fail, **but God** is the strength of my heart." **PSALM 73:26 (NIV)**

GOD TIME

Remember God Math? How about God Time?

For God:

1,000 years = 1 day and
1 day = 1,000 years

Take Moses. God chose him as a great leader—but not until he was eighty! Or what about Abraham? God gave him a baby—but not until he was one hundred!

Or Jairus's daughter. Everyone wanted Jesus to rush-hurry-quick HEAL her before she died—but Jesus stopped to heal an old lady.

"You're too late!" everyone told Jesus. But remember God Time?

Jesus's delay saved an old lady. And meant he didn't just heal the little girl—he raised her from the dead!

Does it seem like God has forgotten about you?

If God is delaying, it's not to make things worse. It is always only so he can make things better.

"My times are in your hands." **PSALM 31:15 (NIV)**

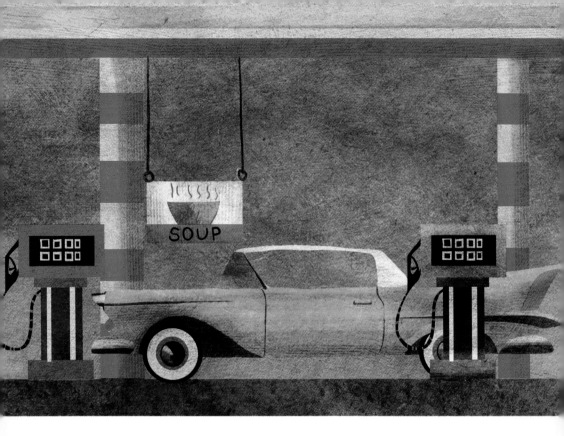

CARS

What if you put porridge in a car's tank? No!
Bad idea!

How about tomato soup then? Stop it! The car
won't run properly—actually, it won't run AT ALL!

The Bible says if we put anything in the center
of our lives except God, we won't work properly
either.

We are built for love and joy—not for sin and tears.

The Bible says only God understands the human heart and how it works best—after all, he made it.

And the one who made your heart can also mend it.

"He has sent me to heal those who are brokenhearted."
ISAIAH 61:1 (GWT)

BORN TO FLY!

Have you seen eagles teaching their babies to fly?

Oh dear. Poor eagle babies. Imagine one minute you're all cozy in this warm, lovely nest and the next, you're being pushed out—BY YOUR OWN PARENTS!

But the parents know what they're doing.

As the babies plummet, they flap their wings in a panic—and grow stronger. The parents catch them on their wings and lift them back up, over and over, until at last the baby learns to do what it was born for—FLY!

And the Bible says you were ment to fly as well—to soar in God's love, trusting him, loving him. You were born to fly!

"Those who trust in the Lord will find new strength. They will soar high on wings like eagles."
ISAIAH 40:31 (NLT)

WINTER

In the winter it looks like the trees have all died. Their leaves wither and drop off. They stand like skeletons against the cold, desolate sky.

But did you know before even a single leaf falls to the ground, next spring's bud is ready? Next summer's leaf is furled inside that tiny bud, waiting.

And Jesus says there is nothing broken that won't be mended, nothing sick that won't be healed, nothing dead that won't live again. Because God is making everything sad come untrue!

We can't see it now—but remember the fruit tree in winter? It looks dead. But the buds are ready to go. And come spring—blossom and fruit!

[Jesus said,] "Look, I am making everything new!"
REVELATION 21:5 (NLT)

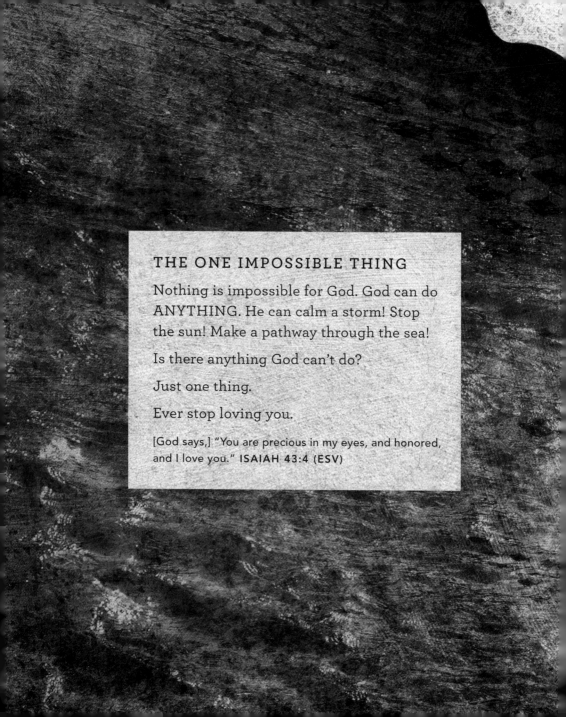

THE ONE IMPOSSIBLE THING

Nothing is impossible for God. God can do ANYTHING. He can calm a storm! Stop the sun! Make a pathway through the sea!

Is there anything God can't do?

Just one thing.

Ever stop loving you.

[God says,] "You are precious in my eyes, and honored, and I love you." **ISAIAH 43:4 (ESV)**

BY THE HAND!

When you're in the dark or on a narrow path, you need someone to lead you by the hand, to hold your hand tight. You need someone to rely on.

God says we can rely on him:

> I've got you by the hand
> And I'll never let you go!
>
> No matter where you go,
> No matter what you do,
> You always have
> A hand to hold you.
>
> I will lead you,
> Guide you,
> Keep you.
>
> Even through death
> I won't ever let you go!

"I will take you by the hand and guard you."
ISAIAH 42:6 (NLT)

BIBLIOGRAPHY AND SOURCES— (OR MORE THINGS TO THINK ABOUT)

Here is a list of the places where I found the quotes I've used in this book, as well as some other books that have inspired me (aside from the Bible itself) in writing these thoughts.

I've also added some other quotes and books that have encouraged me and which I thought might encourage you too.

DANCE and CATACLYSM

"The motions of the universe are to be conceived not as those of a machine, or even an army, but rather as a dance, a festival, a symphony, a ritual, a carnival, or all these in one. They are the unimpeded movement of the most perfect impulse toward the most perfect object."
C. S. Lewis, *Studies in Medieval and Renaissance Literature*

"Wherever man is made the centre of things, he becomes the storm-centre of trouble." Dorothy L. Sayers, *Letters to a Diminished Church*

"Sin is not a matter of morality or conduct, but a state of orientation of a man's entire consciousness which does not make God its center."
Arthur McGill, *Sermons*

For further reading on the idea of the Dance, pick up:
C. S. Lewis, *Mere Christianity* and *Perelandra*
Tim Keller, *King's Cross*

LOVING HEAVENLY FATHER

This thought was inspired by Amy Carmichael's April 22 entry in *Edges of His Ways*.

GOD'S LITTLE FINGER

This thought was inspired by Tim Keller, who based his illustration on a talk given by Barbara Boyd in the 1970s.

GLORIFY!

"In commanding us to glorify Him, God is inviting us to enjoy him."
C. S. Lewis, *Reflections on the Psalms*

"You will be filled with my joy. Yes, your joy will overflow!" John 15:11 (NLT)

LET THE SUN IN!

This thought was inspired by Amy Carmichael's May 7 entry in *Edges of His Ways*.

FISH OUT OF WATER

"A fish may lie at liberty upon the land and spring about, but it is no where truly free except in the water. That which water is to fish, God is to the spirit." Gerhard Tersteegen (18th century writer), *Select Letters*

GOOD NEWS!

"The Gospel isn't good advice to men but good news about Christ; not an invitation to do, but a declaration of what God has done." John Stott, *Basic Christianity*

ARE WE TROUBLING GOD?

"Some people think God does not like to be troubled with our constant coming and asking. The way to trouble God is not to come at all." D. L. Moody, *Prevailing Prayer*

LIFTOFF

"God created the world out of nothing, and as long as we are nothing, he can make something out of us." Martin Luther

RESTING AND RELYING

"Real true faith is man's weakness leaning on God's strength." D. L. Moody, *The Way to God*

CLOUDS AND MOUNTAINS AND STARS

This thought was inspired by Amy Carmichael's March 27 entry in *Edges of His Ways.*

ACORN POWER

"We may easily be too big for God to use, but never too small." D. L. Moody

HOPE

Jonathan Edwards quote taken from "Christian Happiness" in *Sermons and Discourses 1720–1723, The Works of Jonathan Edwards.*

ARROW PRAYERS

"Faith is the gaze of a soul upon a saving God." A. W. Tozer, *The Pursuit of God*

TO MAKE YOUR HEART SING

"There is not one blade of grass, there is no color in this world that is not intended to make us rejoice." John Calvin, *Selections from His Writings.*

MISSING SHOVEL

Story taken from Ernest Gordon, *Through the Valley of the Kwai.*

BELIEVING AND DOUBTING

"Faith is not merely you holding on to God—it is God holding on to you." E. Stanley Jones, *Abundant Living*

"It is not thy hold on Christ that saves thee; it is Christ." Charles Spurgeon, *Sermons of the Rev. C. H. Spurgeon: 2nd Series*

TRYING AND TRUSTING

"I say: 'Well, then, you are now ready to call yourself a Christian.' And they hesitate. And I know they have not understood. Then I say: 'What is the matter? Why are you hesitating?' And they say: 'I do not feel I am good enough.' [...] They are thinking in terms of themselves; their idea still is that they have to make themselves good enough to be Christian, good enough to be accepted with Christ. [...] But you will never be good enough; nobody has ever been good enough. The essence of Christian salvation is to say he is good enough and I am in Him!" David Martyn Lloyd-Jones, *Spiritual Depression: Causes and Cures*

GOD'S PRESCRIPTION

"God gives men promises to see if they will trust him." Richard Sibbes, sixteenth-century Puritan (source unknown)

"Let God's promises shine on your problems." Corrie ten Boom, *Each New Day*

"Never be afraid to trust an unknown future to a known God." Corrie ten Boom, *Each New Day*

WHY WORRY?

Elizabeth Cheney's poem is called, "Overheard in an Orchard," and can be found in L. B. Cowan's *Streams in the Desert*.

NAGGING GOD

"Thou art coming to a King,
Large petitions with thee bring;
For His grace and power are such,
None can ever ask too much ..."
John Newton, "Come, My Soul, Thy Suit Prepare." Composed in 1779.

THE YOUNG CHAMPION

"What joy did Jesus Christ have to come to earth to win that he didn't already have in heaven?" Tim Keller, taken from his sermon entitled "Self Control," May 30, 2010

SMALL AND SCREECHY

Inspired by John Stott's sermon on "Sparrows: Self Esteem"

RADAR IN FOG

"Faith is like radar that sees through the fog—the reality of things at a distance that the human eye cannot see." Corrie ten Boom, *Tramp for the Lord*

TALK TO YOURSELF!

"Have you realized that most of your unhappiness in life is due to the fact that you are listening to yourself instead of talking to yourself?" David Martyn Lloyd-Jones, *Spiritual Depression: Its Causes and Cure*

FLY YOUR FLAG

"Joy and gladness will be found in her; thanksgiving and the sound of singing." Isaiah 51:3 (NIV)

STILLED STORM

"Oh, Lord … You rulest the raging of the sea: when the waves thereof arise, thou stillest them." Psalm 89:9 (KJV)

SUPERPOWER STRENGTH!

"We grow small trying to be great." E. Stanley Jones, *Victorious Living*

LEAP INTO LIGHT!

John Newton's original hymn, "Amazing Grace," can be found in Olney and Cowper's *Olney Hymns* (1779).

FORGIVEN!

"To forgive is to set a prisoner free. And then to discover that prisoner is you." Lewis B. Smedes, *The Art of Forgiving*

For further reading on Forgiveness, pick up:
Corrie ten Boom, *The Hiding Place*

THE LITTLE BIRD TEACHERS

"You see, he is making the birds our schoolmasters and teachers. It is a great and abiding disgrace to us that in the Gospel a helpless sparrow should become a theologian and a preacher to the wisest of men. We have as many teachers and preachers as there are little birds in the air. Their living example is an embarrassment to us … Whenever you listen to a nightingale, therefore, you are listening to an excellent preacher … It is as if he were saying, 'I prefer to be in the Lord's kitchen.' He has made heaven and earth, and he himself is the cook and the host. Every day he feeds and nourishes innumerable little birds out of his hand." Martin Luther, *The Sermon on the Mount* (1521)

LIKE A DEER

Inspiration for this thought came from Amy Carmichael's March 19 entry in *Edges of His Ways*.

BELIEVE

"I'm not moved by what I see. I am not moved by what I feel. I am moved by what I believe." Smith Wigglesworth (source unknown)

GOD'S GALLERY

"The Spacious Firmament on high,
With all the blue Etherial Sky,
And spangled Heav'ns, a Shining Frame,
Their great Original proclaim:
Th' unwearied Sun, from Day to Day,
Does his Creator's Power display,
And publishes to every Land
The Work of an Almighty Hand.
Soon as the Evening Shades prevail,
The Moon takes up the Wondrous Tale,
And nightly to the list'ning Earth
Repeats the Story of her Birth:
Whilst all the Stars that round her burn,
And all the Planets, in their turn,
Confirm the Tidings as they rowl,
And spread the Truth from Pole to Pole.
What though, in solemn Silence, all
Move round the dark terrestrial Ball?
What tho' nor real Voice nor Sound
Amid their radiant Orbs be found?
In Reason's Ear they all rejoice,
And utter forth a glorious Voice,
For ever singing, as they shine,
'The Hand that made us is Divine.'"
Joseph Addison, "Ode—A Spacious
Firmament," published in *The
Spectator* (1712)

GOD TIME

"God's delays don't make things
worse. They always make things
better." Tim Keller, "A Dying Girl
and a Sick Woman"

CARS

"A car is made to run on petrol, and
it would not run properly on anything
else. Now God designed the human
machine to run on Himself. He
Himself is the fuel our spirits were
designed to burn, or the food our
spirits were designed to feed on.
There is no other. That is why it is no
good asking God to make us happy
in our own way without bothering
about religion. God cannot give us
happiness and peace apart from
Himself, because it is not there.
There is no such thing." C. S. Lewis,
Mere Christianity